WITHDRAWN

D1265223

EXPLORING SPACE

Space Shuttles

by Colleen Sexton

Consultant:
Duane Quam, M.S. Physics
Chair, Minnesota State
Academic Science Standards
Writing Committee

BLASTOFF!
3
READERS

BELLWETHER MEDIA · MINNEAPOLIS, MN

Note to Librarians, Teachers, and Parents:

Blastoff! Readers are carefully developed by literacy experts and combine standards-based content with developmentally appropriate text.

Level 1 provides the most support through repetition of high-frequency words, light text, predictable sentence patterns, and strong visual support.

Level 2 offers early readers a bit more challenge through varied simple sentences, increased text load, and less repetition of high-frequency words.

Level 3 advances early-fluent readers toward fluency through increased text and concept load, less reliance on visuals, longer sentences, and more literary language.

Level 4 builds reading stamina by providing more text per page, increased use of punctuation, greater variation in sentence patterns, and increasingly challenging vocabulary.

Level 5 encourages children to move from "learning to read" to "reading to learn" by providing even more text, varied writing styles, and less familiar topics.

Whichever book is right for your reader, Blastoff! Readers are the perfect books to build confidence and encourage a love of reading that will last a lifetime!

This edition first published in 2010 by Bellwether Media, Inc.

No part of this publication may be reproduced in whole or in part without written permission of the publisher. For information regarding permission, write to Bellwether Media, Inc., Attention: Permissions Department, 5357 Penn Avenue South, Minneapolis, MN 55419.

Library of Congress Cataloging-in-Publication Data

Sexton, Colleen A., 1967-
Space shuttles / by Colleen Sexton.
    p. cm. – (Blastoff! readers. Exploring space)
Includes bibliographical references and index.
Summary: "Introductory text and full-color images explore the function and history of space shuttles in space. Intended for students in kindergarten through third grade"–Provided by publisher.
ISBN 978-1-60014-294-9 (hardcover : alk. paper)
1. Space shuttles–Juvenile literature. I. Title.
TL795.515.S49 2010

Text copyright © 2010 by Bellwether Media, Inc.
Printed in the United States of America, North Mankato, MN.

010110   1149

Contents

Space shuttles are **spacecraft**. They carry people into space and bring them back to Earth.

Space shuttles **launch** from Kennedy Space Center in Florida. Thousands of people prepare a shuttle for launch.

Workers connect a large fuel tank to the shuttle. The fuel powers the main engines during the launch.

Workers connect two **solid rocket boosters** to the fuel tank. The boosters help lift the shuttle into space.

solid rocket boosters

A huge machine called a **crawler** moves the space shuttle to a **launch pad**.

launch pad

crawler

The shuttle crew is ready.
The main engines start, and the
solid rocket boosters roar.

The space shuttle lifts into the air and speeds toward space. The fuel tank and solid rocket boosters break away and fall back to Earth.

The space shuttle **orbits** Earth.
It circles the planet once in
90 minutes.

The space shuttle has three main parts. The front part has the **flight deck**. Pilots sit there to fly the shuttle.

The crew lives below the flight deck. They float from place to place because there is little **gravity** in space.

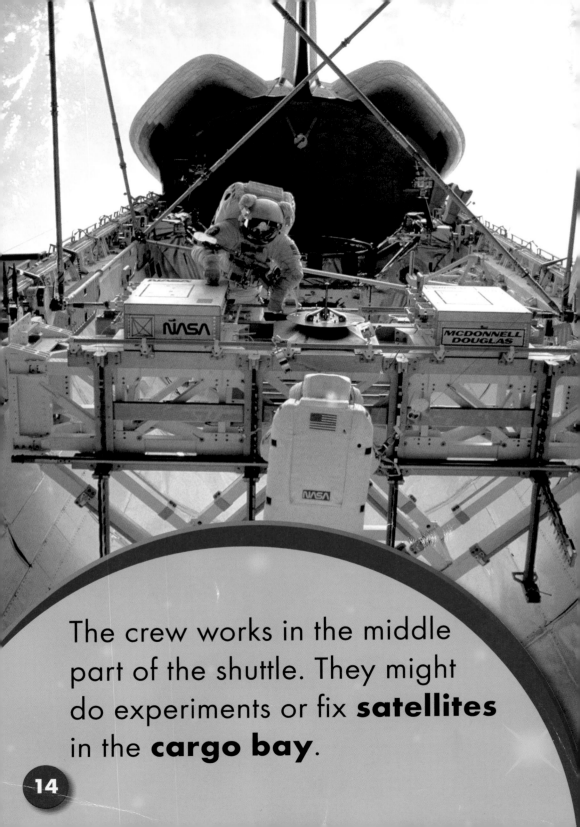

The crew works in the middle part of the shuttle. They might do experiments or fix **satellites** in the **cargo bay**.

The cargo bay doors can open. The crew uses a robot arm to move satellites into or out of the cargo bay.

robot arm

Sometimes the cargo bay carries parts to build or fix a space station.

The back part of
the space shuttle has
three main engines.
It also has two
smaller engines.

It is time to leave orbit.
The pilot uses the small engines
to turn the shuttle toward Earth.

The wings help the shuttle glide through the air. The **rudder** helps it steer.

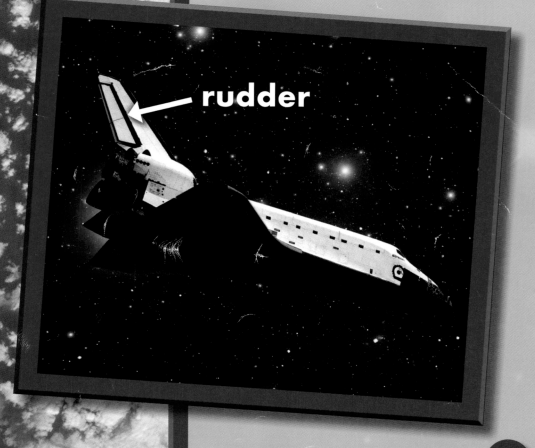

rudder

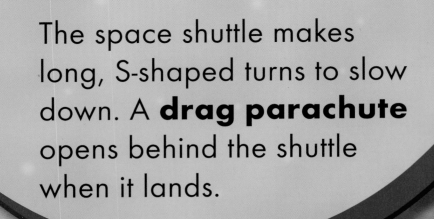

The space shuttle makes long, S-shaped turns to slow down. A **drag parachute** opens behind the shuttle when it lands.

drag parachute

The drag parachute
helps the brakes
bring the space
shuttle to a stop.
The shuttle is
home again.
Welcome back!

Glossary

cargo bay—the large area in the middle of the space shuttle that carries supplies; the cargo bay can also hold satellites and other spacecraft.

crawler—a large, heavy machine used to move large objects like space shuttles

drag parachute—a large piece of lightweight material that connects to the back of a space shuttle; the drag parachute slows the space shuttle during landing.

flight deck—the upper area in the front of the space shuttle where the pilots sit

gravity—the force that pulls objects toward each other; gravity keeps objects from moving away into space.

launch—to send a spacecraft into space

launch pad—a platform from which a spacecraft is sent into space

orbits—travels around the sun or other object in space

rudder—a tall, triangle-shaped part on the back of the space shuttle; pilots use the rudder to help steer when they land.

satellites—objects sent into space to orbit Earth; satellites can help predict weather, take pictures of Earth, or beam TV signals to Earth.

solid rocket boosters—long rockets that help launch a space shuttle into space; solid rocket boosters can be reused.

spacecraft—vehicles that travel in space

To Learn More

AT THE LIBRARY

Bingham, Caroline. *First Space Encyclopedia*. New York, N.Y.: DK Publishing, 2008.

Bredeson, Carmen. *Liftoff!* New York, N.Y.: Children's Press, 2003.

Todd, Traci N. *A Is for Astronaut*. San Francisco, Calif.: Chronicle Books, 2006.

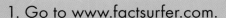

ON THE WEB
Learning more about space shuttles is as easy as 1, 2, 3.

1. Go to www.factsurfer.com.

2. Enter "space shuttles" into the search box.

3. Click the "Surf" button and you will see a list of related Web sites.

With factsurfer.com, finding more information is just a click away.

BLASTOFF! JIMMY CHALLENGE
Blastoff! Jimmy is hidden somewhere in this book. Can you find him? If you need help, you can find a hint at the bottom of page 24.

Index

Blastoff! Jimmy Challenge (from page 23).
Hint: Go to page 11 to catch a ride.

10